Sι

12 Rules For Life – An Antidote For Chaos

EpicRead

© 2018

Contents

What do we see when we don't know what we are looking for?

The construction of soul and world

Rule #11; do not bother children when they are skateboarding

The patriarchy: help or hindrance?

Rule #12; pet a cat when you encounter one on the street

No matter how restricting a set of rules may seem, it is true that without them we quickly become slaves to our passions-and there is nothing freeing about that. In this book, the rules are supported by stories which help us understand why they are needed. The author also explains why the best rules do not restrict us but instead facilitate our goals, making for fuller and freer lives.

The author, Professor Peterson, is described as a knowledgeable but down to earth person who talks like he is thinking out loud and seems to care about a thought only if it might, in some way, be helpful to someone. He also did statistical research on personality and temperament and had studied neuroscience. The author's previous book, "Maps of Meaning", shows his wide-ranging approach to understanding how human beings and their brain deals with any situation that arises whenever something happens in our lives which we do not understand.

The rules in this book have an element of universality to them because we all have to deal with the unknown and we all attempt to move from chaos to order. One of the most important themes of this book is, 'set your house in order' first and the author provides practical advice on how to do this. Rules are demanding and they stretch you to a new limit but without them life has no meaning.

The ancients also discovered that different civilizations had different ideas on how to practically live life, but it did not paralyze them. On the contrary, the modern society became divided into relativism (a concept that everything, including rules, are relative to a person and their circumstances), nihilism (complete rejection of all religious beliefs and morals) and ideology (a simple-minded I-know-it-all approach to life). The author, in this book, has created a sort of 'guideline' for life inspiring from ancient wisdom that has been preserved over hundreds of years against all odds.

Chaos and order are the yin and yang of this world. Just when things seem secure (order), the unknown can loom, unexpectedly and large (chaos). Conversely, when everything seems lost, new order can emerge from catastrophe and chaos. Its no wonder that people will fight to protect themselves from something that saves them from chaos and terror.

We need to stay on the straight and narrow path that lies between order and chaos since the extremes of both of these are destructible. Each of the twelve rules in this book and the accompanying essays provide a guide to being there. This dividing line is where we are stable enough, exploring enough, transforming enough, repairing enough and cooperating enough. Its here that we find the meaning that justifies life and its inevitable suffering.

Rule #1-Stand up straight with your shoulders back

This chapter starts with the example of lobsters and wrens, both of which are ferociously protective of their home territory. Both are also obsessed with status and position, like a great many creatures. Also, wrens and chickens are observed to have a dominance hierarchy where the strongest, healthiest and most fortunate bird gets the perks of a prime location for home away from wind and rain and has easy access to food. Territory matters and there is little difference between territorial rights and social status. Similarly, when a contagious disease spreads through the birds, it is often the most stressed and least dominant birds that suffer from it. Same is true for humans as it is said that when the aristocracy catches cold, the working class dies of pneumonia. Because territory matters and the best locales are always short in supply, conflicts occur which must be resolved with both parties incurring the least damage. Consequently, the living community has established ways to reduce potential conflict between the dominant and subordinate group members and cease fire without further damage.

The neurochemistry of defeat and victory

A lobster loser's brain chemistry differs importantly from that of a lobster winner. Winning increases the ratio of serotonin to octopamine in the lobster's brain who then adjusts his posture to look tall and dangerous. This lobster is statistically predicted to win again in later combats and dominate its world. It also gets all the attention of female lobsters in his vicinity. The existence of lobsters for more than 350 million years highlights that the brain has the structure and neurochemistry to process information about status and society for ages now. This is in conjunction with the human society where the top 1% have as much loot as the bottom 50%. This rule, also known as 'Price's law', applies to population of cities, the mass of heavenly bodies and the frequency of words in a language as well.

The nature of nature

When something new evolves, it must build upon what nature has already produced. Evolution works through variation and natural selection. Variation occurs because of gene-shuffling and random mutation. Nature, then chooses from among them across time.

It is easy to assume that nature is something with a 'nature', something static. However in reality, nature is static and dynamic at the same time. The nature that selects, what we call environment, transforms itself continuously. The fitness to reproduce offspring and fulfill environmental demand is the criteria on the basis of which nature selects. If we conceptualize this environmental demand as static, then it implies that evolution is a never ending series of linear improvements. On the contrary, as environment changes, the features that make an organism suitable to survive it also evolve. Therefore, the theory of natural selection does not posit creatures matching themselves ever more precisely to a template specified by the world. Additionally, some things in nature change more quickly than others such as leaves change faster than trees and trees change faster than forests. If it wasn't this way, then there would be chaos. The beautiful parts of nature (lush greens) are as realistic as its ugly aspects (AIDS and draughts) but we don't realize this. Another misconception is that nature is separate from cultural constructs that delve in it which is wrong. The order within the chaos and order of Being is all the more 'natural' the longer it existed because nature selected it whether it was physical, biological, social or cultural.

Top and bottom

Our brain has a primordial calculator which calculates where we are positioned in the society. Depending on whether you are male or female and your social status, your life conditions will vary considerably. All in all, the bottom of the dominance hierarchy is a terrible place to be in. if you are at the bottom of this hierarchy, the ancient calculator in your brain will wear you down with stress and you will be in a constant state of readiness to do anything to combat the situation. On the other hand, if your calculator calculates a high score on you, you can afford to be a reliable and thoughtful citizen since you have all that life can offer.

Sometimes this counter mechanism can go wrong with erratic habits of eating and sleeping. Routine is therefore immensely important. it is recommended to wake up every day at a fix time regardless of what time you sleep. This is because the systems that mediate negative emotions are tightly tied to properly cyclical circadian rhythms. The next step is to eat a protein and fat-rich breakfast as soon as possible after waking up to reduce anxious feelings throughout the day. Additionally, there are other habits that disrupt this calculator and cause a complex positive feedback loop. This loop is dangerous because each time it picks back the signal, it amplifies it and the intensification gets to the extent where it can become extremely dangerous. When the medication causes the disease, a positive feedback loop has been established. In case of a bad life experience, the dominance counter can transform in a manner that makes additional hurt more rather than less likely.

Rising up

People are bullied because they can't fight back due to physical weakness. However, people are also bullied because they *won't* fight back due to temperamental compassion, a self-sacrificing nature and the concept that feelings of anger are morally wrong. Such people cannot call forth the genuinely righteous and appropriately self-protective anger to defend themselves. If you say "no!" in no uncertain terms, early in the cycle of oppression, then the scope of oppression will remain bounded and limited.

When these naive people are trained to discover the capacity of anger within themselves, they are severely shocked. However, their fear also decreases and they develop more self-respect. Then, they begin to resist oppression. They understand that they must stand up otherwise they will become genuinely monstrous feeding on their resentment. There is very little difference between the capacity for mayhem and destruction, integrated, and strength of character.

Positive feedback loops, adding effect to effect, can spiral counterproductively in a negative direction, but can also work to get you ahead. Also, emotion is partly bodily expression, and can be amplified or dampened by that expression. If you posture is poor then people will react to you like you are losing. Similarly, if you start to straighten up, people will treat you differently. Standing up tall means voluntarily accepting the burden of being which invokes your nervous system to respond in a completely different manner. You are now ready to take your position in the dominance hierarchy and occupy your territory.

So be mindful of your posture, speak your mind, walk tall and gaze forthrightly ahead. Doing so will not only make good things happen but also make those good things feel better when they do happen. Stand up straight, with your shoulders back and you will be able to accept the terrible burden of this world and find joy.

It is surprising why people do not take their medication even when they know it is critically important for them to do so. This is particularly relevant for patients who get an organ transplant and have to take immunosuppressant drugs to prevent their immune system from attacking the newly implanted organ, one they have waited for so long to get. In fact, people are better at filling and properly administering prescription medication to their pets than to themselves. The important question then becomes; what makes people love their pets more than themselves? The answer lies somewhere in the discussion below.

Just as the scientific world consists of atoms and molecules, the world of experience also has constituents. These comprise of chaos, order and consciousness. It is our eternal subjugation to the first two elements that makes us care less for ourselves and it is the proper understanding of the third that allows us the only real way out. Chaos is all those things and situations we neither know nor understand. It is also freedom and the formless potential from which the God of Genesis 1 called forth order using language at the beginning of the time. Order is, on the other hand, explored territory as opposed to chaos. It's the structure of society and biology. Order is the floor beneath your feet and your plan for the day. In order, we are stable, calm and competitive.

We live in time, as well as in space, which implies that even the oldest and most familiar places retain an incredible capacity to surprise you. Friendly dogs can bite and trusted friends can deceive. Such things are real and they matter. Our brains instantly respond to chaos with simple and hyper-fast circuits maintained from the ancient times. After this initial response comes the slow and more complex emotional response and after that thinking of the highest order comes.

The concepts of male and female and parent and child have been around for millions of years, long enough to serve as vital and fundamental parts of the environment to which we have adopted. These are natural categories which are deeply embedded in our perceptual, emotional and motivational structures. We have been interacting with other humans when we lived, mated and evolved and these humans form part of the environment which selects. Reality itself is whatever we survived with and a lot of that is other humans, their opinions and communities. The categories of social brain with which we perceive the chaotic, non-human world are far older than our species. We appear to have taken that primordial knowledge of structured, creative opposition and begun to interpret everything through its lens.

Order is symbolically associated with masculinity because the primary hierarchical structure of human society is masculine. Chaos is, on the contrary, associated with femininity because it is the substance from which all things are made just like a mother bears children. Chaos is also choosy because of its feminine nature. It is nature as women which has shaped our evolution into the creative, industrious and large-brained creatures that we are, unlike our chimpanzee cousins. This bipartisan conceptual subdivision is also portrayed by most profound religious symbols which show the male/female duality in each one of them. The human brain also appears to reflect this duality. Chaos and order have this same relationship of duality since we eternally inhabit order, surrounded by chaos. We experience meaningful engagement when we mediate appropriately between them; have one foot firmly planted in order and the other in chaos. The subjective meaning that we encounter when we are located precisely on the border of order and chaos is the reaction of our deepest being, indicating that stability is ensured but the expansion of habitable, productive territory of your social, personal and natural self is also in works. It is a place where the terror of existence is under control, but where you are also alert and engaged.

In the third verse of Genesis. A snake appears in serpent form in the Garden of Eden. This is symbolic of the order/chaos dichotomy which encompasses all experiences. However, the worst of all snakes is the eternal human proclivity for evil which is psychological, spiritual, personal and internal. Therefore, there is no possible way to ward off evil and make everything permanently and predictably safe. Even if it was possible, we would become extremely dull without any reason to pay attention to the world around us.

The answer to the question 'why someone would buy prescription medication for their dog and then so carefully administer it when he would not do the same for himself?' lies in the story of Adam and Eve. Eve was tempted by the serpent in the Garden of Eden to eat a fruit that would grant her God-like vision. She then made Adam eat it too and all of a sudden they both were aware of the fact that they are naked and thus extremely vulnerable, so they hide away in shame. When God finds out, he banishes both of them along with the serpent out of the Garden to earth. The answer to the above question, therefore, is that why anyone would take care of anything as naked, ugly, ashamed, frightened, cowardly, resentful and defensive as a descendant of Adam even if that Being is himself? No one is more familiar than you with all the ways your mind and body are flawed. Therefore, no one has more reason to hold you in contempt and to see you as pathetic and by withholding something that might do you good, you can punish yourself for all your failings. Furthermore, human beings have a great capacity for wrongdoing and are fully conscious of this attribute. Given that terrible capacity for malevolent actions, is it any wonder that we have a hard time taking care of ourselves? Who then could be faced with illness without doubting the moral utility of prescribing a healing medication? Christ's archetypal death sets an example of how to accept finitude, betrayal and tyranny heroically and how to walk with God despite the tragedy of self-conscious knowledge. It means not to suffer silently and be victimized by a bully, even if that bully is oneself. You are simply not your own possession to torture and mistreat because your Being is inexorably tied with that of others. This not only relates to the people around us but also to God since you have a spark of Divine in you which belongs not to you but to God. We are low-resolution versions of God. Hatred for self and mankind must be balanced with gratefulness for tradition and the state and astonishment at what normal everyday people accomplish. You are important, as are other people, and have some vital role to play in the unfolding destiny of the world. You are, therefore, morally obliged to take care of yourself.

To treat yourself as if you were someone responsible for helping yourself would be to consider what would be truly good for you. This is not equal to what you want or what makes you happy. Consider the future and think about what your life would be like if you took good care of yourself. You have to articulate your own principles so that no one can take inappropriate advantage of you and must discipline yourself carefully. Keep the promises you made to yourselves and reward yourself. Once you are aware of the hell inside you and decide to aim somewhere else, it will replace your shame and self-consciousness with natural pride and forthright confidence.

Rule #3: Make friends with people who want the best for you

Sometimes, when people have a low opinion of their own worth, they choose a new acquaintance of precisely the type that proved troublesome in the past. Such people don't believe that they deserve any better, so they don't go looking for it. People create their worlds with tools they have directly at hand. Faulty tools produce faulty results. It is in this manner that those who fail to learn from the past doom themselves to repeat it.

Rescuing the damned

People also choose bad company because they want to rescue someone. Although it is only right to see the best in people, not everyone who is failing is a victim and not everyone who is at the bottom wishes to rise. People would argue that Christ himself befriended tax-collectors and prostitutes, but you are not Him. How do you know that your attempts to pull someone up would not instead bring them, and even you, down? Down is a lot easier than up.

Maybe you are saving someone because you are a strong and generous person who wants to do the right thing. But maybe you want to convince yourself that the strength of your character is more than just a side effect of your luck and birthplace and you want to draw attention to your inexhaustible reserves of compassion and goodwill. Real improvement requires more than just talking about it, from both of you. Or maybe you are associating with bad company because it is easier. You and your circle of friends decide not to talk about it but underneath you all know what is going on.

Before you help someone, you must confirm why that person is in trouble. If you assume that bad things just happened to them, you are stripping them of all power whatsoever. It is far more likely that they have rejected the path upwards because of its difficulty. Maybe their suffering is a demand of martyrdom for your resources or to inflict the same misery on you so that the painful gap between both of you could be reduced. How can you befriend a person who has developed misery as a weapon against those who rise upward? Maybe it is their revenge on Being.

It is not that there is no hope for redemption, its just that it is much harder to extract someone from a chasm than to lift them up from a ditch. Maybe you should wait until it is clear that they really need help. Otherwise, it may be assumed that you are in an unhealthy relationship because you are weak-willed and indecisive.

A reciprocal arrangement

Loyalty must not be mistaken for stupidity. It must be negotiated, fairly and honestly. Friendship is a reciprocal arrangement whereby you must not choose someone that makes this world a worse place. Its appropriate to associate with people whose lives would be improved if they saw your life improved. If you are surrounded with people who support your upward aim, they will take you up instead of dragging you down.

This is not easy, so have some courage, use your judgement and protect yourself from too-uncritical compassion and pity. Make friends with people who want the best for you.

No matter how good you are at something, or
how you rank your accomplishments, there is
someone out there who makes you look
incompetent. Inside us dwells a critical voice that
knows all this. However, because mediocrity has
both real and harsh consequences, standards are
necessary and failure is the price we pay for them.
We are not equal in ability and outcome and will
never be.

While many psychologists preach that 'positive
illusions' is the only reliable route to mental
health in a world where things are terrible, there
is an alternative approach. If the internal critical
voice makes you doubt the value of your life and
endeavors, maybe it is time to stop listening to it.
Standards of better or worse are not illusory or
unnecessary. Value judgements are a precondition
for action. Furthermore, every activity comes with
its own internal standards of accomplishments.
Anything can be done better or worse which is
why to do anything is a game with a defined and
valued end which can always be reached more or
less efficiently and elegantly. Standards are
important because if there was no better or
worse, nothing would be worth doing.

The logic of the internal critical voice can be
challenged on many grounds including that it only

has two words to define our efforts; success or failure. There exists no middle ground. Such generalizations are not practicable in a world as complex as ours. There is not just one game to play and succeed or fail at rather each one of us is involved in multiple games. Moreover, you cannot excel in each and every one of these and if you do it means that you are not doing anything new and different. You might be winning but you are not growing which is more important. You also might realize that you are overvaluing what you don't have and undervaluing what you do.

As we grow, we become increasingly individual and unique and the standards that helped us grow in our childhood no longer remain relevant. You have individual preferences and nature. However, before you articulate your own standards of value, you must see yourself as stranger and then get to know you. You must determine what you need from the people around you, not what you *should* need from them. Should might enter the picture because you have social obligations but that does not mean you should become a lap-dog. Consult your resentment, it's a revelatory emotion in terms of what you want from life and people in it. If this consultation shows that there is tyranny afoot, it's time to speak up because silence is a lie in such situation.

Our eyes are always pointing at things we want to see and it is important to see, observe and investigate. However, to see, we must aim, so we are always aiming. We cannot navigate, without something to aim at and while we are in this world, we must always navigate. We always encounter the world in a state of insufficiency and seek its correction. We remain curious even when we are satisfied and live in a framework that defines the present as eternally lacking and the future eternally better. The disadvantage to this foresight is chronic ease and discomfort whereas the advantage is that we can change the world for a better future.

Since we always compare what is with what could be, we aim; either too high, too low or too chaotically. The result is that we fail and become miserable. The problem then becomes, how to benefit from our foresight of a better future and our ability to improve it without making our present lives miserable?

The first step is to take stock of ourselves and find what is broken inside us because we are all broken. The internal critic could play the role of inspector here if you get it on track. However, the findings of internal critic must be taken with a grain of salt. You must understand that perhaps happiness is always to be found in the journey uphill, and not in the fleeting sense of satisfaction awaiting at the next peak. Much of happiness is hope, no matter how deep of the underworld it was conceived.

Once the critic has pointed certain things out, negotiate with yourself to get them right. A little careful kindness goes a long way and judicious reward is a powerful motivator. You must use tricks to get yourself to work on these problems by making promises to yourself and then keeping them. Aim small. You don't want too much to begin with given your limited talents, tendency to deceive, burden of resentment and ability to shrink responsibility. Small bits of amends on a daily basis work as compound interest improving your life drastically over the course of years. Now you are aiming higher and learning to see and what you aim at determines what you see. THAT LAST SENTENCE IS WORTH REPEATING!

What you want and what you see

What we see depends on our aim and surprisingly, we are blind towards all other things. This is partly because vision is psychophysiologically and neurologically expensive. Consequently, we triage when we see and save the fovea, the central high-resolution part of the eye, for things of importance. Unless something pops up right where you are focused, you would practically ignore everything else. That's also precisely how you deal with this complex world, you see things that facilitate your movement forward and detect obstacles when they come in your path but ignore the rest of the world. All this ignored world possesses a truly terrible problem when we are in crisis but doesn't matter when all is well.

Maybe we are unhappy because we are blinded by what we desire and what we really need is right in front of us. When things don't work out, maybe it's time to realize that new things need to be born and some things must be let go on the journey uphill. To retool, to take stock, to aim somewhere better, you have to think it through, bottom to top. You have to scour your psyche. And the solution often means taking more responsibility than you care to take.

We, the Being, have primordial desires that must be fulfilled such as hunger and sexual desire. however, we cannot get everything we want all the time because our desires are in conflict with each other, with other people and this world which is a complex but real place. Thus we must become conscious of our desires, articulate them, prioritize them and arrange them into hierarchies. That makes them sophisticated, moral and help them work with other people and this world. What we see and don't see also depends on our religious beliefs, even if you are an atheist. Our underlying beliefs are reflected by our actions which is why you can only find out what you actually believe by watching out your actions. Our beliefs, and therefore what we value, is a product of an unimaginable lengthy developmental process.

Old Testament God and New Testament God

The God of Old Testament can appear harsh, judgmental, unpredictable and dangerous. Even the authors of the Old Testament asked questions with cautions, concluding majorly that God knew what He was doing. New Testament God is often presented as a different character. He is more kind and wants nothing but the best for us. This appears more optimistic but less believable. No one but the most naive of us could believe that an all-good and merciful Being ruled this terrible world.

Faith is not believe in magic, it is instead the realization that the tragic irrationalities of life must be counterbalanced by an equally irrational commitment to the essential goodness of Being. It is a realization that you have literally nothing better to do. You can attempt at this by keeping aside your old strategies of maneuvering, calculating and scheming and paying attention like you have never done before.

Pay attention

Focus on your physical and psychological surroundings. The three most important questions that you must be asking yourself are; what is it that is bothering me? Is that something I could fix? Would I actually be willing to fix it? If any of these questions answers 'no', look somewhere else. Aim lower and search and find something that says yes to all these questions.

Notice your fear and have some empathy for it. If you find something you can fix, ask yourself what you would require to be motivated to undertake that job. Ask and then listen and don't overestimate your self-knowledge. Let the tasks for the day announce themselves for your contemplation. This is an expression not merely of absolute self-control but of the fundamental desire to set the world right.

Realization is now dawning. You are telling the truth, no longer act as a tyrant, are not envious and frustrated anymore because you have learned to aim low and be patient. You are finding that the solutions to your particular problems have to be tailored to you personally and precisely. You don't care what others are doing because you have plenty to do yourself. Attend to the day but aim at the highest good.

Now you have a heavenward trajectory. Ask and ye shall receive, ask and the doors will be opened.

Ask and you may be offered the chance to change your life completely. Compare yourself to who you were yesterday, not to who someone else is today.

Actually, it's not okay

In our everyday lives, we see too many classic examples of too much chaos breeding too much order and the inevitable reversal. Because parents do not teach their children what 'no' means, the poor child has no conception of the reasonable limits enabling maximal toddler autonomy. Many mothers also fail to teach their young boys respect for women which makes them a subject for hatred by their future daughter-in-laws. The preference of male over female child is not strictly cultural but also has psycho-biological reasons. Sons are preferred because they can engage in exponential reproduction cycles with multiple females.

preferential treatment awarded to a son while he is growing up might result in a more confident and successful adult but it can also mutate into something extremely dangerous. Similarly, there are instances where a child is made an unconscious subject of hatred regardless of their gender.

Everybody hates arithmetic

It is the things that occur every single day that truly make up our lives and time spent the same way over and again adds up in an alarming rate.

Some people think that if there are problems between the parent and child, it is the parent or broader society that is at fault because there are no bad children. This concept is dangerously one-sided, both for parents who are blessed with a difficult daughter/son and the society which is held responsible for all human corruption.

If one believes that society is at fault here, then they try to force a major social restructuring to counter such issues which is not practicable. Each person's private troubles cannot be solved by a social revolution because revolutions are destabilizing and dangerous. Horror and terror lurk behind the walls so wisely put up by our ancestors and we tear them down at our own peril. Today's parents are extremely terrified of their children because they face unfair criticism and the inability to distinguish between the chaos of immaturity and responsible freedom.

The ignoble savage

The eighteenth century Genevan French philosopher Jean-Jacques Rousseau believed firmly in the corruptive influence of society over children. He claimed that nothing was as gentle and wonderful as man in his pre-civilized state. Not to mention that he abandoned five of his children to orphanages noting his inability as a father!

However, the truth is that the mythologically Divine Child permanently inhabits our imagination, as does the darkness that dwells in our souls which is also there in no small part in our younger selves. In general, people improve with age rather than worsening and become more emotionally stable as they mature. Furthermore, there is direct evidence that the horrors of human behavior cannot be so easily attributed to history and society. Chimps have been observed to be capable of great brutality whereas the horrific accounts of destruction of Chinese villages by the invading Japanese also proves that human capacity for self-control might be overestimated. But the evidence strongly suggests that human beings have become more peaceful as time has progressed and societies became larger.

Because children, like other human beings, are not only good, they cannot simply be left to their own devices and bloom into perfection. Children are even more complex than dogs to socialize which is why they are more likely to go completely astray if they are not trained, disciplined and properly encouraged. The vital process of socialization prevents much harm and fosters much good. Children can also be as much damaged by a lack of incisive attention as they are by mental or physical abuse.

Parent or friend

Modern parents are simply paralyzed by the fear that they will no longer be liked or love by their children if they chastise them for any reason. They want to be friends to their children and are willing to sacrifice respect to get it. This is wrong because a child will have many friends but only two parents (hopefully) and parents are more than friends. Therefore, parents need to learn to tolerate the momentary anger of their children when they are corrected.

The responsibility to discipline a child is a combination of mercy and long-term judgement and is indeed a difficult task. Because of this combination, any suggestion that all constraints placed on children are damaging can be perversely welcome. Scientific literature also clarifies another misconception that strict limitations facilitate rather than inhibit creative achievement. Equally ungrounded assumptions entail that children will know exactly what to do if their perfect nature is allowed to manifest itself. The fact is that infants are like blind people and they push the limits to see what is acceptable. They do so to explore, express outrage and frustration which is all very natural. Consistent correction of such actions indicates the limit of acceptable aggression to the child whereas its absence merely heightens curiosity.

Modern parents are also terrified of the two words; discipline and punish, both of which should be handled with care. Both of these are also necessary and there is no escaping their use. Parental interventions that make children happy can and should be used to shape behavior. Additionally, negative emotions like hurt and fear, help us learn just like their positive counterparts. In fact, pain is more potent than pleasure and anxiety more than hope. A careful balance of negative emotions is therefore required to keep us living and thriving which is why we do our children a disservice by failing to use whatever is available to help them learn, including negative emotions. Although such use should occur in the most merciful way possible. It is not important to shelter children from failure to save them the pain but to maximize their learning so that useful knowledge may be gained with minimal cost. Parents who refuse to adopt the responsibility of disciplining their child think they can easily opt out of the conflict that entails being strict but they are exposing their child to even worse than fear and pain. You can discipline your children yourself or you can turn that responsibility over to the harsh and uncaring judgmental world. Every child should also be taught to comply gracefully with the expectations of the civil society. Parents must reward actions that will bring their child success in the outside world and use threat and punishment to eliminate behaviors that will lead to misery and failure. Also, there is a tight window to achieve this so it must be done quickly.

Poorly socialized children have terrible lives which is why it is better to socialize them optimally. It is a very straightforward idea that bad laws drive out respect for good laws. Limit the rules and then figure out what should happen when one of them is broken but remember to use the least force necessary to enforce these rules. The level of 'minimum force necessary' must be established experimentally starting with the smallest possible intervention. To ensure that you children are a pleasure to be around for other people and that you are not disgraced in public by their inappropriate behavior, it is important to know something about reward and punishment instead of shying away from the knowledge.

It must also be noted here that forms of physical punishment are also necessary because the alternative could be fatal. The penalties for misbehavior become more severe as children become adults and it is disproportionately those who remain unsocialised effectively by age four who end up being punished explicitly by society in their later youth. You are not doing your child any favors by ignoring misbehavior. Furthermore, the only time NO ever means NO in the absence of violence is when it is uttered by one civilized person to another. People who argue that hitting a child will merely teaches them to hit ignore the fact that if 'hitting' described the entire range of physical force, then there would be no difference between rain droplets and atom bombs.

Another disciplinary principle is that parents should come in pairs so that when one of them is exhausted by the adversities of life, the other one can step in to observe and discuss. Also, parents should understand their own capacity to be harsh, vengeful, arrogant, resentful, angry and deceitful. People are aggressive and selfish, as well as kind and thoughtful, which is why no one can truly tolerate being dominated by an upstart child. Starting with fewer spontaneous offers of love, this can turn into total familial warfare. Therefore, a parent who is aware of their limited tolerance must have a serious disciplinary strategy in place, overlooked by a more awake partner and never let things go to the extent of genuine hatred. Parents also have a duty to act as merciful and caring proxies of this world. It is more important than ensuring happiness, fostering creativity or boosting self-esteem.

The good child-and the responsible parent

A properly socialized child will be accepted everywhere which will do more for their eventual individuality than any cowardly parental attempt to avoid day to day conflict and disagreement. Do not be afraid to have likes and dislikes when it comes to raising children. Once you have clarified your stance and have assessed yourself for pettiness, arrogance and resentment, the next step is to make your children behave. You take responsibility for their discipline as well as for the mistakes that you will make while doing so. Clear rules and proper discipline make for secure and calm children and parents as well as help the child, family and society establish, maintain and expand the order that is vital to protect us all from chaos.

A religious problem

Whenever we experience injustice or encounter tragedy, the temptation to question Being and curse it rises foully from the darkness. Life is indeed very hard and human control is limited which is why we blame someone or something for our intolerable state. The stupidity of the joke being played on us as mortal Beings motivated mass murders, often followed by suicide. While everyone has different reactions to the harsh brutality of this world, the underlying question always remains to find an answer as to WHY so much suffering and cruelty exists?

Truly terrible things happen to people which is why it is not a wonder that they are out for revenge. But how can the demand for vengeance be distinguished from that for justice? However, people emerge from terrible pasts to do well. The author knows a person who decided to be a good person and then did impossible things required to live that way. The fact that abuse disappears across generations is a testament to the genuine dominance of good over evil in the human heart. The desire for vengeance, however justified, also bars the way to other productive thoughts. The author quotes the example of Aleksandr Solzhenitsyn who reconsidered his life while imprisoned in a Soviet camp. He learned to watch and to listen and let every harmful thing in himself die. He also wrote a book called 'The Gulag Archipelago' which played a great part in crumbling the communist tyranny for good. This highlights that good can also come out of the bad experiences of life. A great many people have adamantly refused to judge reality, to criticize Being and to blame God.

Things fall apart

This is life. We build structures to live in as well as families, states and countries. But when everything goes well, success makes us complacent and ignorant of our surroundings. We fail to notice that things are changing or that corruption is taking root. And everything falls apart. A hurricane is an act of God but failure to prepare when the necessity for preparation is well known, is sin.

Here is something to think about. Consider your circumstances and think if you have taken full advantage of the opportunities offered to you. Have you cleaned up your life? If the answer is no then it is time to stop doing what you know to be wrong. Don't waste time questioning what you know is obviously wrong. Every person is too complex to know themselves completely and we all contain wisdom that we cannot comprehend. It is also important not to overlook your cultural guidelines completely because life is short and you don't have time to figure everything out by yourself.

Stop blaming and don't try to reorganize the state if you can't bring peace to your own household. Let your soul guide you and watch what happens over the days and weeks. Gradually your head will start to clear up as you stop filling it with lies and become genuinely honest with people around you. Your experience will improve as you stop distorting it with inauthentic actions. You will then become to realize other subtle things that you are doing wrong correcting which will make your life even simpler. You will then be left with the inevitable bare tragedies of life which will no longer be compounded with deceit.

If all people did this, the world might stop being an evil place. It might even stop being a tragic place. Who knows what existence might be like if we all decided to strive for the best?

Life is suffering but what in the world should be done about it?

The simplest and most obvious answer is to pursue pleasure and follow your impulses. However, one might think if there is a more powerful and compelling alternative? The answer to this question lies in our ancestral stories but we are not yet wise enough to comprehend the message in those stories. We simply started noticing what we were doing one fine day and then told stories about it. But we didn't and still don't understand what it all means.

After mankind was exiled from paradise and began its mortal existence, the idea of sacrifice emerged which was conceived as a way to divert God's wrath. It meant that something better might be attained in the future by giving up something of value in the present. There is little difference between sacrifice and work. We began to realize long ago that reality was structured as if it could be bargained with. We learned that behaving properly now would bring rewards in the future. The act of making sacrifice was an early and sophisticated enactment of the idea of delay- to wait for a better future. This helped mankind learn sophistication over time, making them more patient and considerate for themselves and others around them. Just like delaying gratification for a better tomorrow dates back several hundred years ago, there are similar long journeys between every leap in sophistication.

The future is a judgmental father. Small sacrifices may be sufficient to solve smaller problems but it is also possible that large sacrifices might solve large and complex problems. So sacrifices are necessary to improve the future and larger sacrifices can be better. Nonetheless, it often appears that sacrifices of high quality are not rewarded by a better future, although it is unclear why.

To share means to initiate a process of trade. According to Benjamin Franklin, asking someone for something not too extreme was the most useful and immediate invitation to social interaction. A productive and truthful sharer is the prototype for a good citizen. Implicit, unrecognized value came first when we acted without thinking (in our animal phase) and it was only through keen observation of thousands of years that humans recognized that the successful amongst us delay gratification. A person who wishes to rectify the flaws in Being and alleviate suffering will make the greatest of sacrifices of everything that he loves. He will forego expediency and pursue the path of ultimate meaning.

Death, toil and evil

The world is set hard against us but man's inhumanity to man is something even worse. thus, the problem of sacrifice is not limited to moral limitation that must be addressed by work but it is the problem of evil as well. Evil enters the world with self-consciousness. Human evil adds a whole new dimension of misery to the world. Conscious human malevolence can break the spirit even tragedy could not shake. Continually rejected sacrifices bends and twists people into truly monstrous forms who then consciously begin to work evil. All of this implies that the central problem of life is not merely what and how to sacrifice to diminish suffering but to diminish suffering AND evil which is the conscious and vengeful source of the worst suffering. Evil amplifies the catastrophe of life, dramatically increasing the motivation for expediency already there because of the essential tragedy of Being. It requires a special sacrifice to beat that evil and it is the description of this special sacrifice that has preoccupied the Christian imagination for centuries.

It was the alchemists who first began to study the transformations of matter in hopes that they could discover the secrets of health, wealth and longevity. Science developed as a consequence. On the other hand, Christianity elevated the individual soul and put masters and slaves on the same footing which is why it will be wrong to say that it was a failure in comparison to science. Christianity made the claim that even the lowliest person had rights and that the state was morally challenged to recognize those rights. It produced a far less barbaric society than the pagans. Only after the most obvious of the problems were eliminated by Christianity came the less obvious ones, the solution to which motivated the development of science aimed at resolving the suffering which plagued the successfully Christianized societies.

In late nineteenth century, a philosopher by the name of Nietzsche emerged who challenged Christianity and the problems left unresolved by the religion on three main grounds. He criticized Christianity for the sense of truth developed by the religion, the fact that it was believed that Christ redeemed all humans and that there was nothing left for anyone else after Him to do and the notion that salvation could not be achieved through works. These beliefs of Christianity implied that only the hereafter mattered, that salvation is impossible to earn in this life through any amount of effort and that it was the right of the believer to reject any real moral burden because Christ had already done all the important work. These are the reasons behind the criticism of Christianity by many philosophers.

However, these philosophers also believed that an individual must be constrained by a restrictive disciplinary structure before they can act freely or competently. A long period of unfreedom and adherence to a single interpretive structure is important for the development of a free mind. But this Christian Dogma is now dead and nihilism has evolved.

The reality of suffering is the only thing that cannot be doubted because it is so real. Even nihilists cannot argue against it. Similarly, inflicting suffering on another person is completely wrong. We do not understand what is good, but we certainly understand what is not. If the worst sin is tormenting others for the sake of suffering, then good is what is diametrically opposite to that. Humility is therefore advised because totalitarian pride manifests itself in intolerance, oppression and torture. Consider the evil in your own spirit before you blame others because maybe its not the world but you who is at fault and above that do not lie. Make it your axiom that you will act in a manner that will alleviate pain and suffering. Expedience is the following of short term gain and blind impulse. Meaning is its mature alternative which can be achieved once you place 'make this world a better place' at the top of your value hierarchy. Expedience is wrong because it merely transfers the curse on your head to someone else or to your future self in a manner that will make your future worse instead of better. Meaning is the ultimate balance between chaos and order and when everything there is comes together in an ecstatic dance of single purpose.

Do what is meaningful, not what is expedient.

Taking the easy way out or telling the truth-those are not merely two different choices. They are different pathways through life. They are utterly different ways of existing. 'Acting politely' means to use your words to manipulate the world into delivering what you want. Its scheming and sloganeering and propaganda. People engaged in such actions are living a life-lie where they attempt to manipulate reality with perception so that only some narrowly desired outcome is allowed to exist. They believe that current knowledge is enough to define what is good and that reality would be unbearable if left to its own devices.

There is another fundamental problem with the life-lie, particularly when it is based on avoidance of things that could be changed if you did something about them. Someone hiding is not someone vital because vitality requires original contribution. If you will not reveal yourself to others, you cannot reveal yourself to yourself. Researchers have recently discovered that new genes in the central nervous system turn themselves on when you place yourself in a new situation. You have to explore new things to get yourself turned on otherwise you will be living the life of an incomplete person.

Of you say 'no' when it needs to be said, then you transform into someone who is capable of saying no. on the other hand, if you betray yourself and act out a lie, you weaken your character. And it is not a vision that is at fault here but willful blindness which is the worst sort of lie. It is prudent to start with small changes but sometimes the entire hierarchy of values is faulty. Error necessitates sacrifice to correct it and serious error necessitates serious sacrifice.

There is no blaming of any of this on unconsciousness either because an individual knows when he is lying even if he pretends to ignore it. And the sins of such an unauthentic individual corrupt and destroy the state. Furthermore, any natural weakness or existential challenge can be magnified into a serious crisis with enough deceit in the individual, family or culture. With love, encouragement and character intact, a human being can be resilient beyond imagination. However, it is the absolute ruin produced by tragedy and deception that is unbearable.

Reason lives in every one of us and sees farther than any other spirit but it falls in love with its own productions, worshipping them as absolute. It is the greatest temptation of the rational faculty to glorify its own capacity and its own productions and to claim that in the face of its

Theories nothing transcendent or outside its domain need exist. What ultimately saves us is not what we know but our willingness to learn from what we don't know. That is faith in the possibility of human transformation.

It is deceit that makes humans miserable beyond what they can bear. It fills human soul with resentment and vengefulness.

The truth, instead

An aim provides a structure for action and without it there would be no meaning to life. It is necessary to aim at your target, however traditional, with eyes wide open. Your direction might be wrong and your plan might be ill-formed. You must remain awake to catch yourself in the act. Culture is always in a near-dead state because the wisdom of past deteriorates or becomes outdated in proportion to the genuine difference between the conditions of the past and present. That is a genuine difference but it is also the case that culture and its wisdom is vulnerable to corruption and to voluntary willful blindness. The act of seeing what is in front of us becomes particularly important when it challenges what we know and rely on. You are not only what you know but also what you could know if you would which is why you should never sacrifice what you could be for what you are. Never give up the better that resides in you for the security of the present and certainly not when you have a glimpse of something beyond. Every bit of learning is a little death which challenges a previous conception.

Set your ambitions even if you are unsure about what they should be. Better ambitions have to do more with the development of character and ability than status and power. If you pay attention to what you say and do, you can learn to feel a state of internal division when you are misbehaving. When you lie, you sacrifice the ability to know if a goal, alternative to what you have, might serve you and this world better. As you continue to live in accordance with the truth, you will have to face conflicts that will help you continue to become mature and more responsible. Your conception of what is important will become more and more appropriate, you will quit wildly oscillating and move more directly towards the good.

In short, everyone needs a goal to limit chaos and all such goals must be subordinated to a meta-goal such as "live in truth'. This means that you should follow the path that takes you to your goal but be open to allow the world and your spirit unfold as you do so.

One of the greatest discoveries of humanity is that things fall apart and we speed up this natural deterioration through our blindness, inaction and deceit. The biggest of lies are composed of smaller lies and those are composed of still smaller lies. On surface, it just seems a misstatement but underneath is hidden its genuine dangerousness and its equivalence with the great acts of evil that man perpetuates and often enjoys. Afterwards comes the arrogance associated with the production of successful lies and finally the proposition that Being deserves no respect because I can fool it. And when reality hits them and things fall apart, the individual becomes bitter and looks out for revenge because they blame the world for their horrendous state. That's the gateway to hell.

Your truth is something only you can tell and depends on no ideology. Apprehend your personal truth and communicate it in an articulate manner to yourself and to others. Truth will keep your soul from withering as you face the inevitable tragedies of life and help you avoid the terrible desire to seek vengeance for that tragedy. Tell the truth-or at least don't lie!

Rule #9; Assume that the person you are listening to might know something you don't

Not advice

Psychotherapy is genuine conversation instead of advice which often means that the person you are talking to wants to revel in the superiority of their own intelligence. Genuine conversation is exploration, articulation and strategizing. Its when you are mostly listening which is equivalent to paying attention. People need to talk because that is how they think and they need to think because it is necessary to simulate the world and plan how to act in it. Also, people think that they think but it is mostly self-criticism that passes for thinking. True thinking is listening to yourself and its difficult. It is an internal dialogue between two or more different views of the world.

True thinking is complex and demanding. It requires you to be an articulate speaker and careful listener at the same time. It also involves conflict which further involves negotiation and compromise. If you are not good at thinking and being two persons at the same time, then you need someone to listen.

A listening person is your collaborator and opponent. He is a representative of common humanity which is why he is typically right. Nonetheless, it is important for the individual to stand up and tell the truth because conflicting opinions sometimes save the humanity from perishing. However, if you are insistent on bending the world your own way, you might have some very good reasons to back it up. Otherwise, you might be in for a very hard landing. You should do what other people do unless you have a very good reason not to.

A listening person

A listening person can reflect the crowd and he can do that without talking. He can do that merely by letting the talking person listen to himself. A good therapist will tell you about what he thinks so you have the honest opinion of at least one person. That is not easy to get and that is not nothing. That's the key to the psychotherapeutic process; two people tell each other the truth and both listen.

According to a great psychotherapist Carl Rogers, it is a great rule to apply when in an argument that no one can speak up for themselves until they have restated the ideas and feeling of the other person. An advantage of this methodology is that you get to understand what the person is saying. Another advantage is that this practice helps consolidate the whole conversation to (hopefully) good memories in the minds of both the speaker and the listener. The third advantage is that this method is that it obstructs the careless construction of straw-man arguments so that you do not oversimplify or distort the position of your speaker.

If you listen, without premature judgement, people will generally tell you everything they are thinking and with very little deceit.

Conversations have other forms which are much less counter-productive and even dangerous. There is a type where people are jockeying for position and even exaggerating for it. Another form is when neither speaker is listening in the least to the other instead they cannot wait for their turn to speak. Yet another form is when one participant is trying to attain victory for his point of view. Genuine listening conversations, on the other hand, occur when only one person is talking and therefore organizing an event in their minds. Every sane mind requires listeners which is why it is the fundamental duty of parents to render their children socially acceptable so they can have people around them who can listen. The sympathetic responses offered during a genuine conversation implies that the speaker is valued and the story is important and serious. In this context, women are often intent on formulating the problem when they are discussing something and they need to be listened to and even questioned to help ensure clarity in the formulation. Then, whatever problem is left, if any, can be resolved.

Another form of conversation is a lecture where the lecturer is talking *with* and not *at* or even *to* his listeners. He must take his listeners as individuals who need to be included in the conversation rather than taking them as an audience. A successful public speaker focuses his attention on one individual after another, responding to them after closely monitoring their emotions and expressions. Funny and humorous conversations are another type that work primarily as demonstrations of wit.

The final form of conversation, akin to listening, is a form of mutual exploration. It allows all participants to express and organize their thoughts and has a topic that is of genuine interest to the participants. Instead of validating their own positions, everyone is trying to solve a problem. All of them are acting on the premise that they have something to learn. Such conversations constitute active philosophy which must be the one with which the participants are genuinely involved in.

Your current knowledge is radically insufficient to make you perfect or to keep you safe. You must accept this before you converse philosophically. For this kind of conversation, you must respect the personal experience of your conversational partners and believe that if they shared their conclusions with you, you could bypass at least some of the pain of personally learning the same things. It is as if you are listening to yourself as you are listening to the other person and it leads both of you to somewhere newer and better. You both change as you embrace your new selves. So listen to yourself and to those with whom you are speaking. Your wisdom will then consist of not only the knowledge you have but the continual search for knowledge which is true wisdom.

Why does complex machines like laptops become obsolete so fast? This is because of the nature of our perception themselves and the invisible interactions between those perceptions and the underlying complexity of the world. Our laptops are just a tiny part of a whole system of technologies and systems efficiently interacting together. So much of what they are resides outside their boundaries that they can only maintain their computer-like facade for a few short years. This is true for everything we see and hold.

Tools, obstacles and extensions into the world

Our evolved perceptual systems transform the interconnected, complex multi-level world that we inhabit not so much into things *per se* as into 'useful things'. This is a practical reduction of the world. We see 'tools' and 'obstacles', not objects or things. Furthermore, we see tools and obstacles at the "handy" level of analysis that makes them most useful (or dangerous), given our needs, abilities and perceptual limitations. When we look at the world, we perceive only what is enough for our plans and actions to work and for us to get by. But the objects we see do not exist independently in this world but exist in a complex and multi-dimensional relationship to one another.

All of this is true for our perceptions of ourselves. The extensible bodies of ourselves expand to include other people and other things. We can identify with a fictional character in a movie or with a whole group in competition. Similarly, we can also identify with our country and might even sacrifice ourselves to defend it.

The world is simple only when it behaves

The conscious illusion of complete and sufficient perception only sustains itself when everything goes according to the plan. For example, we are unaware of the mechanics of our cars until they break down. When our car fails, our incompetence with regards to its complexity is instantly revealed. This has practical as well as psychological consequences. We turn to experts in this case so that the simplicity of our perceptions can be restored and start questioning a lot of things. It is then that the walled garden we archetypally inhabit reveals its hidden but ever-present snakes.

The past is not necessarily what it was and the present is chaotic and indeterminate. Also, the future can change into something it was not supposed to be. Everything is intricate beyond imagination and is affected by everything else. Our perceptions are very narrow and we try very hard to avoid the knowledge of that narrowness. However, this inadequacy in perception is dangerously revealed when something goes wrong.

What we perceive, when things fall apart, is no longer the stage and settings of habitable order but the chaos that is lurking beneath our thin surfaces of security. When things collapse around us, our perception disappears and we act. During these circumstances, our bodies ready themselves for all possible eventualities.

What do we see when we don't know what we are looking for?

Don't ever underestimate the destructive power of sins of omission. Why refuse to investigate, to talk about the elephant in the room, when knowledge of reality enables mastery of reality? Do you truly think it is wise to let the catastrophe grow in the shadows, while you shrink and decrease and become ever more afraid? If you wait instead, what you least want will inevitably happen and when you are least prepared. What you least want to encounter will make itself manifest when you are the weakest and it is the strongest, and you most certainly will be defeated.

Specifying the problem is to admit that it exists whereas avoiding this specification is like failing to define success so you don't have to notice when you fail and it won't hurt. However, the truth is that you cannot be fooled that easily unless you have gone too far down the road. When things fall apart and chaos re-emerges, we can re-establish order through careful and precise speech.

The construction of soul and world

The psyche (the soul) and the world are both organized, at the highest levels of human existence, with language, through communication. The problem must be admitted as soon as it emerges and it must be analyzed if you are being immature or the problem is indeed that grave. We parse the complex and tangled chaos to specify the nature of things because otherwise the damaged machinery will continue to malfunction if its problems are neither diagnosed nor fixed. There is question of difficulty here because the alternative is worse.
Precision specifies. It may leave the tragedy intact but it chases away the ghouls and demons. If you shirk the responsibility of confronting the unexpected, even when it appears in manageable doses, reality itself will become unsustainably disorganized and chaotic. Ignored reality transforms itself into the great Goddess of Chaos. Be careful with your words and organize them into correct sentences and correct paragraphs. In this way, the past can be redeemed, the present can flow by without robbing the future and you can extract the stellar destiny from a multitude of

unpleasant futures. Courageous and truthful words will render your reality simple, well-defined and habitable.

You must determine where you have been in your life, where you are going in your life and say what you mean so that you can find out what you mean. Then act out what you say, pay attention, note errors and strive to correct them. Only this can protect you from the tragedies of life.

Be precise in your speech.

Rule #11; do not bother children when they are skateboarding

People, including children, don't seek to minimize risk. They seek to optimize it. Thus, if things are made too safe, people (including children) start to figure out ways to make them dangerous again. We prefer to live on the edge which is why we are hard-wired to enjoy risk. Overprotected, we will fail when something dangerous, unexpected and full of opportunity suddenly makes its appearance, as it inevitably will.

A study of deep psychologists reveals that there is a dark side to everything. The psychologist 'Jung' produced the most wicked psychoanalytic dicta, 'if you cannot understand why someone did something, look at the consequences, and infer the motivation'.

We deserve some sympathy for the hypothetical outrage of our destructive behavior because we have only just developed the conceptual tools and technologies that allow us to understand the web of life. We do what we can to make the best of things and the planet is harder on us than we are on ourselves. Nonetheless, human beings are remarkable creatures and its unclear if they have any real limits. Mountain bikers, freestyle snowboarders and skateboarders do tricks all the time that seemed humanely impossible before.

Mass murderers are driven by a near-infinite resentment for humanity which encourages them to eradicate it and act as sort of heroes. Even their own Being does not justify the existence of humanity and they kill themselves to justify the purity of their commitment to annihilation. The male members of the society have been particularly targeted by this philosophical berating which deems their accomplishments unearned and portrays them as sexual suspects. Boys are suffering in the modern world because they are stubborn and tough. Schools do not accept provocative behavior no matter how competent it might show a boy or girl to be. Also, boys are reluctant to play girls' games and find themselves in a terrible position when competing with a girl where they can neither win nor lose without negative consequences. It costs them their reputation to be good at something that girls value. The situation in universities is also not encouraging as almost 80% of students majoring in the fields of healthcare, public administration, psychology and education, are females. This is bad news for both boys and girls.

The percentage of men declaring that a successful marriage is one of the most important thing in life is declining as opposed to females, where this is a popular opinion. Why it is then that career has become more important than family and love when money fails to improve people's lives beyond a certain limit? This is because this increases their desirability in the eyes of female partners (and potential partners) who prefer a spouse with a desirable job.

The increasingly short supply of university-educated men is posing a serious problem for females who want to marry or date and don't have time to do so because of their highly demanding careers. Furthermore, marriage is becoming increasingly reserved for the rich. Women want an employed partner of a preferably high status because they want to compensate for when they bear children and become more vulnerable. So, the unemployed working man is an undesirable specimen and single motherhood is an undesirable alternative. The problem is further exacerbated by political correctness in universities where whole disciplines have been forthrightly hostile towards men.

The patriarchy: help or hindrance?

Culture is an oppressive structure, of course, but it also takes with one hand and gives more with the other in some fortunate places. Although it must be subject to criticism, culture is not something that should only be taken as oppressive and ignorant. Absolute equality would require sacrifice of value itself because it is the desire to work towards something valuable that renders life meaning and creates hierarchies. And any hierarchy creates winners and losers.

Culture is also symbolically, archetypally and mythically male but it is the creation of humankind rather than just males. Women were treated differently, legally and practically, before the twentieth century because they had to face certain things that were unknown to men such as menstruation, unwanted pregnancies and limited physical strength. There are also examples of men like Muruganantham, Simpson and Haas who freed women from some of their vital troubles such as lack of sanitary pads to be used during menstruation and birth control pills. Are all these male oppressors part of the patriarchy culture as we believe it?

The disciplines which that teach young people that our incredible culture is the result of male oppression are heavily influenced by Marxist humanists. These humanists believed that Western principles were plagued with inequality, domination and exploitation. We have all seen the negative consequences of the adoption of Marxism in China, Vietnam, Cambodia and other countries in the form of miserable life of the citizens in these societies.

Despite the atrocities of communism witnessed and heard of in the Soviet Union, the attitude towards it remained consistently positive among many Western intellectuals. Nonetheless, some eyes remained open such as those of George Orwell and Aleksandr Solzhenitsyn which utterly demolished communism's moral credibility.

The French philosopher, Jacques Derrida, was of the view that hierarchical structures emerged only to include the beneficiaries of that structure and to exclude everyone else. It is almost impossible to overestimate the nihilistic and destructive nature of this philosophy. It puts the act of categorization itself in doubt. It negates the idea that distinctions might be drawn between things for any reasons other than that of raw power. However, power is a fundamental motivational force but the fact that power plays a role in human motivation does not mean that it plays the only role, or even the primary role. Likewise, the fact that we can never know everything does make all our observations and utterances dependent on taking some things into account and leaving other things out. That does not justify the claim that everything is interpretation, or that categorization is just exclusion.

It is also true that not all interpretations are equally valid. Some hurt while others are not sustainable across time. Some of these constraints are built into us and some emerge as a result of increased socialization. All in all, an endless number of interpretations exist that can be quoted as a seriously bounded number of viable solutions because life is not easy.

The author personally thinks that the remake of university administrations into analogues of private corporations is a mistake. He does not understand why public funding is made available to institutions whose aim is to demolish culture that supports them and to propagate the notion that all hierarchies are based on power. Historical and current data suggests that societies that are well-functioning have competence, ability and skill, as opposed to power, as the main determiners of status. Thus, not only the state is supporting one-sided radicalism, it is also supporting indoctrination.

The insane postmodern concept that society must be altered, or bias eliminated, until all outcomes are equitable merely implies the use of force. Moreover, the introduction of 'equal pay for equal work' complicates even salary comparisons for people occupying the same positions beyond practicality. Who decides what is 'equal work' or 'who is disabled?' or 'what racial categories are real?' every person is unique and group membership cannot capture that variability.

It is a completely wrong idea to teach boys to be compassionate like girls, however, their aggressiveness must be sophisticated temperamentally to avoid rejection by peers when they are no longer kids. Similarly, many females have family and job problems because they are extremely compassionate and not aggressive enough. The Disney stories such as 'The Little Mermaid' tell us that for a woman to become complete, she has to embrace the masculine consciousness (which does not always involve a man) and stand up to the terrible world. An actual man can help her do that but it is better for everyone if no one is too dependent. When softness and harmlessness become the only consciously acceptable behavior, then hardness and dominance becomes an unconscious fascination. This means that if men are pushed too hard to feminize, they will become more interested in harshness. Men have to toughen up because men demand it and women want it. This is why boys perform dangerous skateboarding tricks and quit classrooms to work in difficult conditions. And if you think tough men are dangerous, wait until you see what weak men are capable of.

Leave children alone when they are skateboarding.

The studies of social psychologist Henri Tajfel demonstrated that people are social as well as anti-social. They are social because they like the members of their own group and they are anti-social because they don't like the members of other groups. Both cooperation and competition are socially and psychologically desirable which is why being social and anti-social are both important. People favor the groups which thrive because they want to climb up the dominance hierarchy and climbing something which is failing is not a useful strategy.

A superhero who can do anything turns out to be no hero at all. Be must have limitations to meet the expectations of his fans who can only relate to him as long as the limitations making his story possible are coherent and consistent. Being of any reasonable sort appears to require limitation. Perhaps Being requires becoming as well as mere static existence and to become is to become something more, or at least something different. That is only possible for something limited.

But with limits comes suffering which the Being is entitled for their lifetime. When existence reveals itself as existentially intolerable, thinking collapses in on itself. In such situations, it is noticing (not thinking) that does the trick.

If you pay careful attention, even on a bad day, you may be fortunate enough to be confronted with small opportunities that bring extra light on a good day and a tiny respite on a bad one. Such opportunities may involve a cat on the street that accepts your patting graciously or a little girl dancing on the street because she is all dressed up in a ballet costume. And maybe when you are going for a walk and your head is spinning a cat will show up and if you pay attention to it then you will get a reminder for just fifteen seconds that the wonder of Being might make up for the ineradicable suffering that accompanies it.

Pet a cat when you encounter one on the street.

Conclusion

Thank you again for downloading this book!

I hope this book was able to help you to get more insight to all the key components of the book in less time.

The next step is to try out the practical approaches listed in this book and find the ones that work best for you.

Check out the Audiobook in Audible too

Just wanted to say thank you once again for purchasing and reading my book.

I truly do appreciate it!

Best Wishes,

EpicRead

Made in the USA
Coppell, TX
03 July 2020